Pain Tried to Bury Me Alive

But God Revived Me

A Memoir

Author Jessica M. Harris

Scriptures marked KJV are taken from the KING JAMES
VERSION (KJV): KING JAMES VERSION, public domain.

ISBN: 9798426077058 (Paperback)
ISBN:9798436086903 (Hard Cover)

Dedication

I dedicate this book to my three children Tiana, Kai and Tariq. May each of you continue to excel and reach for the stars in everything that you do. God has a purpose for you and I am grateful to have a front-row seat to all of it. Each of you were brought into my life at a pivotal time. God knew that I needed each of you on this journey. Mommy loves y'all very much.

Acknowledgments

First and foremost, I have to give all the Glory and Honor to God. He has truly had his hand on my family and I. Time and time again, I have been able to witness the magnitude of God's love, His presence, His grace and His mercy. In these moments, I appreciate the relationship that I have been able to build and cultivate over time. If it wasn't for God keeping me, I truly don't know where I would be right now. He saved my life, my mind, my body and my soul.

Thank you to my parents Iris and Tony Harris for loving me and encouraging me. Thank you to my brother and sister Tony Jr. and Amaris for always being ready to love on my children when I would do surprise visits. My children truly adore y'all.

To the many friends and family members who have walked with me on this journey, I thank you. I appreciate you for showing up when it was needed the most. 2021 was a year of ups and downs, but I am grateful for all of it because everything that I endured has built me to be the person that I am today.

Table of Contents

A Toast to You Moving Past Your Pain...

I need you to know that where you are right now is not your final destination.

I need you to know that God planted a purpose within you and if you let Him in, He will cultivate the space needed for your purpose to grow. God created you and your life experiences shaped you. Some of those experiences shaped you so much that you got lost in them and forgot who you were. Your life became all about your kids, your spouse, your job, your past, your pain and more. So, what happened? Where did your goals and dreams go? Where did your hope and joy go? Not every person gets caught up in this journey, but this toast is for the ones who did. Everyone's journey is different. Trust and know that God sees you and He is waiting for you to come to Him. It's your turn. There's so much life that is left inside of you. Do you dare to take a step into where He is calling you?

You are beautiful/handsome.
You are more than your past mistakes.
You are bold and filled with wisdom.
You are needed in this world

Keep pressing forward and keep moving your feet. You got this. Cheers! Today is a new day filled with new opportunities. Peace and blessings to you and your family.

-Jessica Harris

About the Memoir

Being myself, a girlfriend, a mom, an employee, a daughter and more were all roles and positions I played in life. Somehow, when these worlds met, I started losing myself in the process. Instead of trying to get from under the roles and positions, I played in my life, I was continuously buried instead. Buried underneath the hardships of balancing motherhood, my job, my relationship, and my life.

It wasn't until my ten-year relationship ended that I saw just how broken and lost I was. When it ended, my life unraveled and I didn't know where to put the pieces. I couldn't get to the "me" who needed to come up for air. She was buried too deep. Lost and confused, I called on God to intervene. There was no way I would be able to do this alone because I had no clue how.

This memoir details the journey of healing that God wants for you. He no longer wants His children to be hurt and broken, but to become healed and made whole. The love of God is expressed by devotionals and poetry that God has laid on my heart to share with you. I believe that as you walk through my journey, you will get the revelation that you need for your own.

I encourage you to keep a journal and pen to answer the journal prompts and to write down any revelations you have as you read. God wants to use you. There are people who need you. Take time to really get into the word of God and allow Him in to pour into you.

For there is no respect of persons with God.
Romans 2:11 KJV

God didn't just heal me for me. He healed me so that I could be in a position to share my testimony with you so that you could walk free from pain life has thrown your way. Trust and know that He is able. Allow this memoir to encourage you as you walk in your own healing journey.

Prayer

Lord, I thank you for taking the time to cover me, to heal me, to protect me and to move in my life. I surrender everything unto you. I lay down my burdens at your feet. I ask that you soften my heart and open my mind so that I may be able to receive all that you are doing for me, through me and with me. I pray that I am obedient to what you are calling me to do. I ask that you forgive me of my trespasses and help me to forgive those who have trespassed against me. Continue to renew my mind within you Lord so that my thoughts will be your thoughts. In Jesus' name, I humbly pray.

Amen.

Part I

God is Going to Uproot

the Weeds in Your Life

Chapter 1

Everything Doesn't Last Forever

A Look Behind the Scenes

Have you ever had that one month where something big always happens regardless of the year that you are in? Well for me, that's the month of February. Something big always happens in February without fail. Sometimes it's something good and sometimes there's a twist, but I can't wait to see which one it will be this time. Last year it was me finding out I was pregnant with baby #3. I'm not pregnant this time, so, I wonder what it'll be.

That being said, my name is Jessica, and I am the mom of three small children. I have been in a relationship for the last ten years with their dad and I can say we have had our fair share of ups and downs, but what relationship doesn't? Things have been a bit bumpier over the last few months because we have a newborn again in our home and that means many sleepless nights if you know what I mean.

One of the biggest stressors we've been facing as a family lately was the aftermath of our youngest child being diagnosed with a rare autoimmune disease called Cold Agglutinin Disease (CAD) at two months old. Although he is home recovering with us there are a lot of appointments that still take place throughout the week. So being on our toes with him has taken its toll on all of us. That's not including raising our two older children. Tired and stressed is one way to put how we have been feeling, but I think we're starting to get the hang of it. At least that's what I thought until the day of the argument.

The Argument

I sat on the couch with tears streaming down my face as my head sat in the palms of my hands. I can't put into words what just happened. All I know is that I went into the bedroom after dropping the kids off and I asked my boyfriend a question regarding the kids. That question spiraled into an argument which landed me sitting here on the couch in tears. All I could do was replay what just happened.

I walked into the house and started to pick up some of the things the kids had left out from the day before. My boyfriend saw me walk in and started to mutter something under his breath as he walked into our bedroom, but I couldn't hear him clearly.

So, I went into the room to ask him to repeat what he just said.

I asked, "Can you repeat that? I didn't hear you."

He turned around and boldly said, "I'm tired of always having to repeat   myself."

Now, my hearing is not always the best due to listening to loud music and having a case of selective hearing at times. But today, I really didn't hear him and his response wasn't an actual answer and the attitude was unnecessary. Again, I repeated, "What did you say? And why do you have an attitude? I didn't hear you."

He was clearly frustrated and started to mutter again under his breath. As I got ready to ask him once more about his attitude and why kept speaking under his breath he looked me and said loudly, "I'm done with this."

I looked at him sideways and said, "What do you mean, you're done with this?

He looked up at me shaking his head with his hands in the air, "I'm not doing this anymore. I'm good."

"Okay", I said still confused at what he meant. "What exactly are you done with?" I asked.

This time he put his phone down and looked directly at me and said, "I'm done with all of this. I'm done with you. I'm good on all of it. I'm too young to be this stressed. I'm good."

There was a pause because I was still trying to absorb everything he just said.

Then he continued, "This is not about today or right now. I have been good on you. I was supposed to break up with you on your birthday to be real. But yeah, it's over. I'm all set."

I honestly wasn't expecting those words to come out of his mouth. As they did the tears started to flow down my face and I couldn't stop them.

I looked at him angrily and asked, "Are you serious right now?

He turned around with a blank expression on his face as he shrugged his shoulders back. There was no smile, no tears or any sign of regret on his face. Just him staring back at his phone as though what he said didn't just crush me. I stared at him intensely for a few seconds trying to figure out if he was going to budge or maybe tell me he was joking, but he didn't. All the love that was once in the air vanished into thin air. His demeanor was now cold and crisp. Could it really be over just like that? From the same man who had nothing but love in his eyes the day before. Where did all the love go?

Fed up with the news he just gave, I shouted back, "You knew that if you did not want me, all you had to do was say so. You knew I was not the one to be strung along. Then you want to talk about breaking up with me on my birthday. How were you going to do that? Because I remember quite clearly that you were telling me about your plans for us to get married. So exactly when were you going to break the news to me that you did not want to be with me? Or better yet, were you going to tell me?"

His only response was him shrugging his shoulders.

So, I followed up with, "Why didn't you just end it when you first wanted to be done? Why did you continue? What was the point? I've always made it clear that if you are done then be done, but don't string me along."

At this point, I was in his face shouting because I needed answers. The only response he gave was the shrugging of his shoulders.

In a crisp and cool tone, he said, "None of that matters because I'm good on you."

I couldn't stop shaking my head because this did not make any sense. How did we go from me asking a simple question to breaking up? All the while, he just laid there on the bed with his phone in his hands as he continued to scroll on whatever app he was on. As he scrolled, so did I. But mine was through the last decade. Those years felt like a waste of time and energy. My twenties were gone in the wind with a man who no longer wanted to be with me. I felt robbed and I couldn't get that time back.

<u>The Aftermath</u>

Ugh!
I want to scream!
How could this be happening to me?
Raising kids is hard and I have three,
with all the responsibility falling on me.
How did I even get here?
Sitting on a couch full of tears,
weighing my options sitting in fear.
No clue on what to do or where to go.
No idea on what the future holds.
For me, a newly single mom of three,
unsure of how this could be.
This wasn't supposed to be my story!
It was supposed to end happily,
with me marrying the love of my life.
But at this point,
who would that even be?
Am I worthy of having someone love me?
To hold me, to cherish me.
To treat me like his queen.
I mean this last relationship,
has done a number on me and my self-esteem.
How am I supposed to come back from this?
Is it even possible to meet my king?
A man who understands and can see,
that there is more to me than the broken pieces
that lie before me.
Or will I always be single with the three mini versions of me?

I can't do this.
I can't think.
My head is spinning, and the thoughts keep coming.
I can't breathe like this.
God, why is this happening to me?
The aftermath of it all
is starting to catch up to me.
Weighing heavily on my chest,
waiting to see what is going to happen next.
I just need to leave and gather my thoughts.
I just need to leave so I can take a deep breath.
Deep breath in and deep breath out,
hoping to slow down my mind
Since it's still racing.
~End~

Chapter 2

God Heard My Cry

The Car Ride

I jumped in my car
and took off driving.
In a direction I didn't know,
but I knew I needed to keep going.
To get as far away as I possibly could.
I needed room to breathe
because his words and my thoughts
were suffocating me.
I was drowning in my tears and fears of the unknown.
Questioning God, why I was feeling all alone?
Why was this happening to me?
My tears are growing stronger,*
making my vision blurred.
This is a deathly combo on the road.
God, I need you to take the wheel.
Ahhhhhhhhh!
I screamed!
Today has been a day.
One that I would love to forget.
I can't believe their dad did this to me.
Where does that leave me, God?
Help me Lord and put my mind at ease.
Remind me of your perfect peace.
Can you dry these tears,
and soothe my fears?
I need you God.

I need you.
Deep breath in and a deep breath out.
Deep breath in and a deep breath out.
My breathing is starting to slow down
The tears are almost gone.
I look up to God and whispered thank you.
Because He heard my cry.
~End~

My Shower Prayer

It had been a few hours since I left out of the house. I took a deep breath as I walked up the three flights of stairs to our apartment. I didn't know what I was going to say when I walked through the door. Thankfully my kids were playing in their room and their dad was on the porch. I quickly grabbed a change of clothes from the bedroom and headed into the shower. I needed to be with my thoughts before I could face them. The peace I had earlier started to subside when my thoughts began racing again. Hopefully, this shower could wash away some of this anger and pain because right now, I can't even stand to look them in the face.

I locked the door and turned the water on. I turned the temperature up as hot as I could bare it. I just need a few more minutes to get myself together. As I got in the shower, I kneeled to pray. Just like a dam bursting, all the tears started to fall accompanied by uncontrollable sobs. I couldn't hold back any longer. My heart was aching, and I didn't know what to do or what to say. All I could do was cry as the hot water hit my back. I cried until it felt like there were no more tears left inside.

As I started to regain my composure, I heard God whisper, "He is not your husband." I looked up with a confused look on my face.

Before I could respond, God whispered once more, "He is not your husband." I looked up again and asked, "But why? Why would you let me have three children with him, but not marry him? Why did you let us last this long?" All I could do was shake my head. It didn't make sense.

As my thoughts continued to erupt, God reminded me that I never asked Him, if their dad was who I was supposed to be with. He reminded me that he was a choice I had made all on my own without his input.

As I sat back and started to understand where He was going with this, I knew what He meant. I was shocked at how simple it sounded because it was true. I didn't consult God when I got into this relationship at eighteen. I thought I was an adult and that I could do what I wanted to do. I never knew that I was supposed to consult Him about who I chose to date. If I had, I would have been able to save some time I thought as a small smile crept across my face. At that moment, I knew I was going to be okay. I wasn't sure how, but everything didn't seem as bad because there was still hope for me.

Chapter 3

There's Still Hope

Be ye not unequally yoked together with unbelievers: for what
fellowship hath righteousness with unrighteousness? and what
communion hath light with darkness?
2 Corinthians 6:14 KJV

A few days after the breakup, I found myself sitting with God seeking
to gain a deeper understanding of what was going on in my life. On
one of those nights, a scripture dropped in my spirit, and I realized
why we broke up from God's perspective. What looked like a horrible
situation was really his protection. He was uprooting me from him
because our relationship did not serve His purpose.

God revealed to me that my relationship with their dad did not
have Him at the center. He couldn't be apart of it, because both of our
beliefs were not rooted in God. I believed in God, Jesus and the Holy
Spirit (The Holy Trinity), but their dad did not. My jaw dropped when
I realized that this was even in the bible. All this time, I thought that
him and I having different beliefs would be okay, but God made it
very clear that it was not. He needed me to be one with Him and that
who He had for me would also be one with Him. God didn't want
anything that was not of him to taint me any longer. To be honest, it
sucked to think about, but it made sense. I couldn't stay mad at their
dad for breaking up with me because it really wasn't Him. It was God
placing a wedge between us on purpose.

God knew me well. He knew I would only leave the relationship
if I was put into a position where the choice was not mine. The
betrayal I experienced was not surface deep, it was to keep me from

going down a destructive path. This was a door that needed to close so new ones could open.

Journal
What doors has God closed in your life, so that you could get on the path He has called you to?

Prayer
Lord, I thank you for the doors that you have closed and I thank you for the doors that you are opening. I thank you for always keeping my best interests at heart even when I could not see it. I ask that you continue to soften my heart and renew my mind in you as I continue this journey. In Jesus' name, I humbly pray.
Amen.

Chapter 4

A Quick Rewind of 2020

I wanted to take some time to reflect on how good God is. That even in the midst of storms He has always proven to help me through. I know 2021 is off to a rocky start, but this isn't the first time God has shown up. Here's a look at some of the hardest moments I faced last year. If I could make a list of things to skip, these would be it.

Top 5 tracks to skip in 2020
- Coronavirus pandemic (That might be on everyone's list)
- The world shutting down and schools closing in March.
- Family and friends catching coronavirus including myself.
- The Great Debate: To send or not to send my children back to school
- The baby almost dying from a rare autoimmune disease called Cold Agglutinin Disease (CAD) at two months old.

I ended 2020 exhausted with the hope of a better year to come in 2021. Not everything was bad. There were some lessons I learned along the way like valuing the importance of spending time with family. As well as learning to appreciate not only the big things, but also the small things life offers. The wind got knocked out of me a few times, but I was able to still stand on the promises of God. Just like we may have some bad days, there are still plenty of good days that follow us. Here's a list of moments that I will cherish forever.

Top 6 jams of 2020
- Finding out I was pregnant with baby #3 and having him in the summer of 2020

- Rebuilding my relationship with my children
- Hearing God's voice. He said, "You can't give up."
- Watching God save my baby's life. This was a miracle.
- Having the summer off for the first time in 14 years
- No longer working over 60 hours a week

I added an extra jam on my list because God really came through for my family in 2020 in so many ways. I just needed to give Him the Glory. Because storms will happen, but He always makes a way.

Chapter 5

He Will Always Make a Way

Fear thou not; for I am with thee: be not dismayed; for I am thy
God: I will strengthen thee; yea, I will help thee; yea, I will uphold
thee with the right hand of my righteousness.
Isaiah 41:10 KJV

God doesn't want you to look at your situation and see no way out.
He wants you to see that He is the way out. He is the one who knows
the end from the beginning. When my two-month-old went into the
hospital, I had no clue what was going to happen. All I knew was that
he almost died. It was the words God spoke to me that night that have
been my strength since that day. In the softest voice ever, I heard Him
say, "You can't give up now." I had no clue that the strength He was
pouring into me this night was going to pull me through the months
up ahead when my relationship ended. God doesn't send us into
battles he has not prepared us for.

Journal
Reflect back on how God has shown up throughout your life. Keep a
daily record of these instances so you may be reminded of how good
He is. This will also encourage you to build your trust in Him.

Prayer
Heavenly Father, thank you for always being by my side. I thank you
for not leaving me when things got rough. I thank you for keeping me
when I was at my lowest. I ask that you continue to strengthen me
during my storms so that I may weather them. I trust that you will

bring me through just as you have done for me in the past. In Jesus' name, I humbly pray.
Amen.

Chapter 6:

Who Am I?

After the break-up, I was lost and confused. For the longest time, I was wrapped up in being a girlfriend, a mom, a friend, an employee and more. But who am I? These were just roles, titles and positions I had. I needed to figure out who Jess was. I've lived in a world blended with all these things for so long that I did not know where to begin to uncover my identity. People could see my talents a mile away, but there was still an internal struggle of wanting to fit in and not knowing how.

A Seed Planted
Like a seed planted in the ground,
I was planted and buried deep inside.
Waiting for something to happen.
Waiting for my roots to sprout.
So this shell could bust open.
Never understanding that there was a process.
A need for good soil to be around me.
A need for the right amount of sunlight and water to be given to me.
Just when I believed I had enough of those things,
To grow into something.
The earth would shift
and the land would run dry.
Causing me to stay inside.
Inside of my shell with no roots springing forth,
until they knew that there was a good source.
A source of nutrition to carry me through.

Not just for this harvest,
But for the replanting too.
You see,
my seed was the answer to a need
for generations to come.
It was connected breakthroughs
and the breakings of generational curses.
My seed was connected.
Connected to various lives
and people who needed me,
to not only survive
but to thrive.
To thrive in this world,
without the weeds holding me back '
and keeping me down.
They needed me to rise above the ground,
but this was going to be a process.
Not for the faint or weak at heart.
God needed a willing heart,
so, He could plow the ground
and uproot the weeds.
From all the things that no longer concerned me
mentally, spiritually, physically and emotionally.
He was far from done with me.
There was a renewing of the land
that was taking place.
He was using this as an opportunity to show me,
Just how much he loved me.
The land I was in would no longer run dry,
because He was refreshing the soil with an endless supply
of all of Him and less of myself.
I would forever be connected to one and only source.
Praise be to God for counting this seed of mine to worthy

but he wasn't surprised.
See He knew me,
before I was even formed
in the womb of my mother's belly.
He knew the greatness that was planted within me.
He knew the journey that I would endure
and because He knew,
provisions were made.
Not to scare me, but to show me His grace
And that He and His love will always remain with me.
~End~

At a time when my life looked like it was falling apart, it was really God setting the stage for many breakthroughs to come. He knew that in order for me to grow, I needed to be healed and made whole.

But now, O LORD, thou art our father; we are the clay, and thou our potter; and we all are the work of thy hand.
Isaiah 64:8 KJV

As a human, you live life unaware that the experiences you have endured both good and bad not only shape you, but they shape your perspective. Because so much of the world has tainted you, your identity gets lost in the process.

If you took playdough and rolled it in a field you would find fragments of grass, dirt, and anything else in there sticking to it. If you are going to still use it then you have to pick all that extra stuff out of it. You are just like that piece of clay with the grass and dirt in it. God sees it and wants to remove those things out of you and out of your life. When He is done removing those things, he starts to mold you so that you can be restored to the position He created you to be in.

The beauty of God being a gentleman is that He will never do anything to harm you or force you to do anything. If you choose Him, you can be sure that He will bring the best version out of you. So, don't be shocked when you are feeling out of place. Just know that He is processing you. During that time seek His face and His intentions for you. Renew your mind in Him and allow Him to provide you the clarity on why some parts have to be uprooted. Be willing to have an open heart and an open mind. Do the work that He is requesting of you. As you dive deeper into Him watch how the dirt and grime start to fall off of you. You will start to feel brand new.

Journal
Play worship music for 10-15 minutes and ask God to show you who you are to Him and how does He see you right now? Write down what you see, hear or that which comes to mind.

Read The story of seeds Luke 8:5-15 KJV
Reflect on where you are now in your own journey. Be honest with yourself.

Prayer
Lord, I thank you for uprooting me from the people, places and things that no longer serve me or you. I thank you for your love, your mercy and your grace. I thank you for thinking of me always. I know that it feels uncomfortable right now, but I trust that you are making a way. In Jesus' name, I humbly pray.
Amen.

Chapter 7:

Do You Trust Him?

A Big Leap of Faith

The last Friday in February,
God spoke to me.
He said, "I need you to put your trust in me.
I need you to take a big leap of faith."
Now God and I have been on this walk
for quite some time,
but I had no idea what He had in mind.
As the day passed by while I was at work,
I noticed that my spirit
just would not rest.
There was a roaring in my belly
as I sat at my desk.
Not understanding why
I didn't feel at rest
I got up a few times,
But it would not stop.
God, what is happening?
I can't figure this out.
I stood back up ready to leave
And my spirit said,
"Take everything you need."
Hmmm…
Why do I get the feeling
that I'm not coming back?
Back to my 9-5,
where I've spent most of my time.
God, I need this job

to take care of me and mine.
The responsibility of raising
the three mini versions of me
Falls on me
so how am I going to provide?
How will we ever survive?
God, what are you doing?
I grabbed my belongings
and went outside.
I got in my car
still wondering why
I had this urge to leave
and not come back.
It wasn't until I turned left
That it all made sense.
This was the big leap of faith
That I needed to make.
As I drove away
My spirit settled down
I was at peace
and there was no roaring sound.
A bit confused about what to do
or where to go,
I parked in a lot and
called on God.
Explaining the bills that I knew were due,
asking Him how I was going to make it through?
His only response to me was,
"Do you trust me?"
I pondered and said yes.
I had to believe
that he was going to take care of the rest.
Talk about tests.

This was a big one,
but I had to do it.
God had been showing up for me
Time and time again.
It was only right that I trust Him.
He hasn't failed me or forsaken me.
He's never given me a reason
not to believe.
But this right here,
happened unexpectedly.
I knew I was on a journey of uprooting
people, places and things,
but my job God?
That was a turn of events
that I didn't see coming.
~End~

The truth is my leaving that day was an answered prayer. My youngest really needed me as he was still recovering from being hospitalized in September. I was already attending weekly back-to-back appointments while working full-time in the office. To be honest, it was starting to take a toll on me. This felt like the break I needed, so I could focus on him and his healing. He was regaining mobility and strength in his limbs. His recovery required appointments with early intervention specialists, neurology and hematology/oncology. Needless to say, I was still going to be busy without going in to work.

Journal
Listen to praise worship music for 15 minutes. Ask God where is He leading you next on your journey. Write down what comes to mind including what you see and hear.

Prayer:

Lord, I thank you for trusting me to take this leap of faith. I ask that you continue to build up my trust in you and to show the things you need me to do. I give you control on all the areas concerning me and I ask that you soften the hearts of those around me so that they may understand what you are doing with me. Give me the courage to stand on all the things you are asking of me. In Jesus's name, I humbly pray. Amen.

Chapter 8

Walking in Faith

For we walk by faith, not by sight.
2 Corinthians 5:7 KJV

Walk with Him

I'll never forget the day,
I heard God's voice.
I didn't know what to do
Or what to think.
All I knew
is that the baby was in respiratory distress.
He had lost too much blood.
All I could think of,
will today be the day he takes his last breath?
The doctors had no clue of what was going on
Why was this happening God?
In the midst of tears and fears
God whispered,
"You can't give up now."
But who knew?
The power in the words spoken to me,
telling me to keep fighting
would be giving me strength five months later.
I saw the way He pulled my son through
And I just knew
that if I continued to walk by faith
and not by sight

that he would pull me through this new journey too.
Not having a stable income scared me,
But having a God who is able to perform miracles
empowered me.
I knew that my faith was getting ready to level up,
And that's okay
Because we already built trust.
On a foundation of a promise
that I get to see grow up daily
with new strength and new breath
each and every day.
Against all the odds
that were stacked up against him.
~End~

Journal
When was the last time you had to walk by faith and what did that
walk look like?

Prayer
Lord, I thank you for always showing up in my life. Thank you for
the little and big ways that you are there for me. Thank you for guiding
the right people my way on my journey of learning more about you.
Thank you for aligning me with those who have walked with you so
that I may be encouraged by their testimonies. I pray that my walk
with you also inspires others to follow you. In Jesus' name, I humbly
pray.
Amen.

Chapter 9

Lean into God and Not Your Own Understanding

Trust in the LORD with all thine heart; and lean not unto thine own understanding. In all thy ways acknowledge him, and he shall direct thy paths.
Proverbs 3:5-6 KJV

When I said yes to God about leaving my job, that meant that I was surrendering myself to Him. Living a surrendered life was new to me. I had to learn that surrendering myself included my mind, body and soul. That meant not doing some of the things I was used to doing including going to old methods I had for providing for my family. Job applications were either sent back with them moving on or I just didn't hear back from them. Attempting to use driving apps or food apps came with a hard no as well. Every door I used to use was shut down.

When God said lean into His understanding, he wanted me to let go fully. I used to be what some would say a workaholic. I worked well over 50 hours a week between all the jobs I had for a long time. That was because my parents taught me that hard work paid the bills. I had to unlearn that mindset and learn that God has a better way for me. This took time and it didn't happen overnight. The more I stopped doing what I was used to, the easier it became to follow His lead. It's like dancing. We both can't lead. In this case, God is the lead and we have to learn to submit to His steps and trust that He already knows the path that we should take.

When you lean on God, you are resting in Him. Ask Him to show you what that rest looks like for you in this season. Just know that the more you submit yourself to God and surrender your ways, the more you will start to see the changes take place in your life.

Journal
Listen to soaking/worship music for 15 minutes and ask God, how does he want you to submit to Him? Write down what comes to mind including what you hear and see.

Prayer
Lord, I thank you for this day. I thank you for allowing me opportunities to build my trust in you. I ask that you reveal to me the cracks in the foundation of my trust with you. May you fill them in and seal them, Lord God. So that I may be able to give you my full surrendered yes. I thank you for your patience when I tried to do things by my own hands. I thank you for your grace and the mercy that you show me each day. In Jesus' name, I humbly pray.
Amen.

I Surrender to You

I surrender to you
all of these things
both bad and good.
I open my heart
in plain view,
hoping you understand how serious I am.
I want to be healed throughout my mind.
I want to appreciate this new ride.
I don't want old wounds bleeding on new seats.
I've done that already.
and by the looks of it,
these wounds are pretty deep.
I thank you for saying Yes to my Amen.
I thank you for keeping me
even when I was not in alignment and disobedient.
You still loved me,
and your love didn't keep track or keep score.
It didn't blame me when things got rough.
It didn't make me want to run out.
Instead, it showed me kindness, patience and peace.
It brought newness and joy every morning and in my sleep.
So today I surrender to you
my mind, my plans, my children and my healing.
I know that without you, I can't go past the ceiling.
There's a box that I'm in
and I can't get out.
I can operate inside, but It's getting too small.
In this space you have
nurtured me, fed me, and loved on me.
In return, I have grown.
I have grown in ways that I didn't think were possible.
I have leveled up in areas that I didn't think were for me.

Layers peeled off that I thought would always be apart of me.
You have done more for me than anyone.
So why would I go back?
Back to that crouched position,
where my knees hurt, and my back ached.
This box is getting too small.
I can no longer stand up the way I used to.
I am too big for this box God.
Help me!
Help me move past my insecurities.
Help me see that there was purpose in the struggle.
Show me why you have created me.
Move me out the way, So I can be whole.
Lord over my life
I surrender my expectations of how things will go.
I surrender my hard-headed moments and my complaints.
I can hear your soft whisper "Go and be bold".
Be bold enough to stand up tall.
Trust that if you just stand up the box will go away.
So I lean towards your voice and I adjust my position.
I close my eyes and I think of all your promises.
I take a deep breath and I take your hand.
You said that if I trust you then I'll be able to stand.
So here I am, eyes still closed.
Unaware that I am not in the same spot as I once was.
Unaware that you have placed me on center stage.
Unaware that my blind trust
brought me much further than I could have imagined.
~End~

Part II

Time to Dig Up the Past

Chapter 10

Heal Through Your Words

He healeth the broken in heart, and bindeth up their wounds.
Psalm 147:3 KJV

<u>Intimacy with God</u>

Sitting in the dark shadows of the hallway
with a pen and paper to write
And a flashlight to see.
God this was our time for just you and me.
Waking up in the wee hours,
while everyone was asleep.
Renewing my mind and heart with you,
sitting by your feet.
You filled me up,
with all that I needed.
New plans and strategies
since each day
was a new battle for me.
You uncovered the tools
I thought were lost.
You refined them
and demonstrated to me
how to use them
most effectively.
Because the battles we face
are not against flesh and blood,
but against dark principalities.

That's why there is a strong need
for your people to read
and understand the word for themselves.
Life and truth live within the pages
bringing on new revelations
on a day-to-day basis.
But are they willing to build
an intimate relationship with You?
So, You can share Your wisdom
that You freely give to anyone who asks.
Not hidden, nor kept secret
just looking for an open and willing heart
To receive it.
So take some time and sit by His feet.
The invitation is open.
It's not restricted to only me.
The access is in you
by the way of the Holy Spirit
~End~

Use Your Tools to Heal

See,
some don't open the bible
because they think it's boring.
But the truth is
that its filled with stories and testimonies
of how God shows up just in time.
See there was Joseph,
who had dreams of him ruling everything,
but his family couldn't believe it.
His brothers were filled with so much envy
that they sold him into slavery.
But God, still fulfilled the promise.

Then there was Esther.
She was the apple of the king's eye
with her beauty.
She was made aware that a doctrine
was going to kill her family.
She fasted and prayed before risking her life,
believing that if God was on her side
then she would not die.
There was favor on her life.
Then there was the widow named Ruth
who provides hope
for so many women.
Because she stewarded her singleness
in a way
that was pleasing to God
and in the process Boaz found her.
See the stories we read
can relate so much
to who and where we are in our journeys.
The word of God is not just about the past,
but about how it comes to life in our present.
The word of God is happening all around us,
but are you willing to surrender
to see it in its fullest beauty?
Will you come out of the distractions of the world,
to witness the ever-evolving love story?
Of how God comes after His children
in their hurt and dark place
to heal them and make them whole.
To provide them the tools
so they can go
and share the good news
of what God is able to do.

Not just in their life,
but in the lives of others too.
He openly invites us to spend time with him.
In prayer, fasting and meditation.
In singing, praising and worshipping.
In reading his word and journaling.
Don't just limit God or yourself to these tools
but allow Him to invite you in.
In any way He deems fit.
God is a limitless God,
who can defy the odds
in so many ways
if you just gave Him a chance.
He proves this every day,
when new breath enters your lungs,
but it's up to you to thank Him.
To thank Him for all that He has done
and what He is doing.
Even thanking Him in advance for all He is about to do.
When you understand the love God has for you,
and who you are to Him
you'll walk different.
You'll talk different.
Because the love you have for yourself
will look different.
There's no way that you will be able to remain the same.
You'll have no choice, but to change
because He is renewing you,
in your mind, body and soul.
Those old wounds you once carried
anger, betrayal, rejection and pain,
will no longer be able to rule over you.
Or have a stronghold on you.

Because His love for you conquers all.
The inner work that you will do
will deliver you
from those things and more.
It will no longer feel like its burying you,
but you will be able to rise above the pain.
In ways that you didn't think were possible.
All because of the tools
He unlocked in your toolbox.
So, continue to use them,
have Him refine them
and upgrade them.
As your season changes,
so does their use.
Stop setting limitations
on what they can do.
God is your source of wisdom.
God is your source of truth.
God is your source of healing
and God is always with you.
~End~

My Brokenness Was an Opportunity

Being in a backslidden state,
didn't keep God from speaking to me.
It didn't remove the love that He had for me.
Instead, he used my pain as an opportunity
to come get me,
to come check on me
to come invite me back
with open arms.
Back into His grace,
he fought for me.

He took the time to show me,
that the more I was in His face
he would show me all of His ways
And make a way in the process.
No longer seek perfection
was His order,
but to look at the progress.
His words remained true then
and true now.
Taped to my walls
for the days that I fall
back into the old me.
But not too far
where He can't get a hold of me.
God, keep me in the times of my misery
when my world seems to be crashing all around me.
When the hate spewed my way
tries to toss me,
back and forth day by day
by those who once used to love me.
Keep me God in your perfect peace
as I navigate the streams of these muddy waters
with the tip of my pen.
Creating a new world for my children and I to live in.
Releasing the pain with each stroke I make,
starting new chapters
without the hurt, rejection and blame.
God, you have given me a way,
To communicate to the inner me
and to talk to the younger me.
The one who needed to be loved differently,
So, she could receive her healing.
See,

My pen carries weight.
One that brings on change.
So, the enemy
is pretty pissed with me,
because there is healing
with each stroke I make.
Getting free,
unapologetically.
Meditating on the word of God
And allowing it to fill me
and the voids that have existed in my life.
To heal the wounds that were deep inside.
God hears me.
God sees me.
God speaks directly to me.
My pen is just one of the many tools
God uses to speak to and through me.
His words bring clarity
and opens minds to new heights.
Trading in old lens
for new sight.
Sit still to receive your download,
but patient enough for it to upload.
To be used in the ways in which you are told.
Don't misuse the gifts God gave you.
Steward well and watch Him elevate you.
~End~

Journal

Listen to worship/soaking music for 15 mins. Ask God to reveal the areas where pain, betrayal and past hurts still exist. Also, ask God to reveal the tools that you need to use in this season and ask Him to refine them for you so that you may be using them to their maximum capabilities. Write down all that comes to mind including what you see and hear.

Prayer

Lord, I thank you for the healing that you are doing inside of me. Continue to reveal to me the areas where work is still needed. Show me how to be more like you. Help me to seek you more so that I may have a greater understanding of your word. May your peace that surpasses all understanding be upon me, and every area of my life. In Jesus' name, I humbly pray.

Amen.

Chapter 11

Naked Before God

"Before I formed thee in the belly I knew thee; and before thou camest forth out of the womb I sanctified thee, and I ordained thee a prophet unto the nations."
Jeremiah 1:5 KJV

"we are more than conquerors through him that loved us. For I am persuaded, that neither death, nor life, nor angels, nor principalities, nor powers, nor things present, nor things to come, Nor height, nor depth, nor any other creature, shall be able to separate us from the love of God, which is in Christ Jesus our Lord."
Romans 8:37-39 KJV

My Naked Truth
When I bared my soul to God,
as naked as it could be
I had to realize He hadn't seen.
I mean
He's the one who formed me in my mother's belly.
He already knew all about me.
From my trouble to my past
To My hurt and to my pain.
He knew my wants and my worries
all just the same.
Baring myself wasn't for Him to learn,
But for me to see.

That I was starting to trust Him
with everything dealing with me.
That I could give Him my burdens willingly
because I knew that He was going to
take care of me.
He needed me to bare my soul
because He needed me to see me
uncovered by it all.
Uncovered by the façade I wore all-day,
pretending that everything was okay.
He needed me to see me
both the good and the bad.
To know that there was no point in hiding,
because He was my dad,
my father, my Abba.
I needed to see my current reality,
before continuing on my new journey.
One that would require me to show up consistently,
to knock down the walls surrounding me.
These walls were not placed by God,
But placed by me.
They were done in my hiding
to keep me locked in
away from the hurt
the world did to me.
Keeping me safe
from all who wanted to get to me.
But was I really safe with the walls I placed up?
Was I really doing myself any good,
Keeping those who knew me out?
Only to be upset
when it felt as though I had no friends left.
Being naked in front of God

meant those walls had to fall.
In doing so
I could examine better
the love God had for me.
He said that I was a conqueror
and that nothing in life or death
Nor my past or present
Or any creature would keep Him from loving me.
So, my walls must fall
for me to feel the full extent of love
He had for me.
~End~

Journal
What are some walls you have placed up?

Prayer
Lord, I thank you for coming into my life. I want to give you my unreserved yes to do everything you need to do to restore me. Tear down the walls that I have built Lord and soften my heart. Open my mind so that I may be able to receive all that you are doing in my life. Thank you, God, for not letting me go and for always holding on to me. Today I am releasing everything that has been holding me back. In Jesus' name, I humbly pray.
Amen.

Chapter 12

My God is Bigger

But the Comforter, which is the Holy Ghost, whom the Father will send in my name, he shall teach you all things, and bring all things to your remembrance, whatsoever I have said unto you.
John 14:26 KJV

A Precious Gift
One of the most precious gifts
Jesus left behind
when He died and rose again
was the gift of the holy spirit.
The ability to speak directly to God
that lives within us.
A powerful source
that many forget to acknowledge.
Seeking pastors, preachers and prophets
But forgetting that they too have direct access.
Don't reject the access God has granted you.
A way for you to receive breakthroughs
without always having to find it
in a human or a building.
Cry out directly to Him
And give Him permission
To move within you.
Don't be afraid of the feelings that may rise,
they are coming up for a reason.
Let Him be your teacher

In every season.
To show you that your tears
are not only filled with pain
But that they are
the mode of transportation used to release
The things within you that no longer align.
So that you may gain
insights and wonders
along the way
to your past,
to your present
And all that has taken place.
So let tears flow like a river down your face
as the burdens on your back
Start to fade away.
Just know that God is working,
and that He is truly bigger than any problem
You are facing.
He is bigger than any mistake
You have made.
He is bigger than any demon
that tries to tell you differently.
For His word says
now unto him that is able
to do exceeding abundantly
above all that we ask or think,
according to the power that worketh in us.
God is truly our power source.
Take our power back from the world
and speak life back into yourself.
May the flood gates burst open within you
So, He can replace
every nook and cranny of you

still living in the limited view of what man
thinks belong to you.
Remember that as He fills and humbles you,
he is far greater and far bigger than anything that
comes your way.
~End~

Journal

Soak and worship for 15 minutes with worship music. Ask God to show you the self-limiting beliefs that you have come into agreement with. Write what comes to you including what you see and hear.

Acknowledge and repent for these vows you have made. Ask God to restore you in these areas. Ask Him to direct you to scriptures for you to meditate on.

Prayer

Lord, I thank you for the breakthroughs I have had and for the ones that I will have. I thank you for releasing me from every stronghold that once held me. I thank you for the revelations you have given me. I ask that you continue to direct my paths on this journey. In Jesus' name, I humbly pray.
Amen.

Chapter 13

Speak Life

Death and life are in the power of the tongue: and they that love
it shall eat the fruit thereof.
Proverbs 18:21 KJV

1 on 1 session
My breakthrough sessions with God
included me, Him and my negative self-talk
Most times in my car
While I was out and about
Thinking of where I was and why things were going south
I didn't think I was worthy of having good things
Or good enough to believe in my own abilities
God had to talk to me and straighten that out
It was breakthrough after breakthrough
That took place in my car
So many areas that God needed to minister life back into me
From past relationships
To how I felt about myself
To the way I allowed people to treat me
God was delivering me
But it was going to take time
For me to really believe
But He was determined to get me to see
That if I spoke life into myself and unlearned my thoughts
There were great things in store for me'
I just needed to come from my old ways of thinking

49

And self-limiting beliefs
So I could finally put on
The God-given mindset He had for me
It was a big transition for me to see
life from the other side of surviving
Life had so much more for me
and when I spoke it,
I got to see it
In visions and dreams
And just like Joseph
I knew these would become a reality for me
I just needed to believe in my own abilities
Cultivating the right mindset
so when it was time for these to grow
There would be no weeds getting in the way
because the work was being done now
To dig up the past of all the things
that once got in my way
Healing had to take place
So the fruits of my lips
would match the desires of things being done God's way
~End~

Uncover Your Light

Your words have power.
They can either breed life or take it away.
What is said is formed in your beliefs
and in your thoughts each day.
When you understand that
you start to see how much life you throw away
by your negative self-talk.
There is so much life and light inside of you,
but they are buried under what life threw your way.

Dig up the dirt from around them
And hand them back to God:
your trust issues. mommy issues and daddy issues,
your rejection, abandonment fear, and pain
your anxiety, depression, anger and betrayal.
Not to mention
the old memories hidden in the deep dark corners of your past
along with any other burdens you may have.
Shed the unnecessary weight
that's no longer yours.
Speak out against the silence
that's muzzled your words.
Allow God back in
to speak into those dry bones.
May the words He gives you
rejuvenate your soul.
~End~

Journal

Write out 5-10 positive affirmations regarding different areas of your life. I want you to look yourself in the mirror as you say these out loud. I want you to do this daily in the morning and before bed. Post these affirmations on your mirror or wall so you can see them throughout your day.

Write down the areas where negative self-talk exists. Ask God to heal you in these areas.

Meditate on Deuteronomy 28:1-14 KJV daily

Prayer

I ask that you help me to use my words wisely and that I understand how much power lies in the tongue. I thank you for correcting the

words that I say and the way that I think. Thank you for changing my mindset to yours. In Jesus' name, I humbly pray.
Amen.

Chapter 14

Forgive Daily

Wherefore I say unto thee, Her sins, which are many,
are forgiven; for she loved much: but to whom little is forgiven, the
same loveth little.
Luke 7:47 KJV

Repent

God is our father who loves us, but He has no problem correcting us. During my intimate times with Him, he would show me my ugly side and highlight the areas where I needed to be humbled. I would be sitting in the hallway shaking my head at the memory He was showing me because it was me. There was no denying it. I had to repent then and ask God to forgive me for many things that I had done and that's a daily task. No one is perfect, so daily repentance is a must. As I repented, I asked God to correct my ways. I didn't want to continue doing the same things that were displeasing to him.

Forgive Them Anyway

Forgive the ones who have thrown dirt on your name.
Forgive the ones who have tried to put you to shame.
The ones who openly reject you and blame you,
it's time to forgive them for their ways.
Forgiving them is not about what they did
Or the wrongs they have caused,
but about allowing your heart not to be hardened
by the way, they made you feel.

It's about choosing to love
despite the anger and bitter feelings.
It's about having a God who loves you so much
that it covers a multitude of sins.
Not for you to go back out and do it again,
but to remind you that you are not perfect.
Yet, there is nothing that will stop Him
from covering you, from loving you, from being right by your
side.
So why do you criticize those who have hurt you?
When God is right,
love conquers all.
A lesson to learn is that the love God offers
has been instilled inside of you
to be able to offer
that same love back unto others.
Understand that there are levels to love
and not everyone will comprehend,
But you do.
You know the love that God has for you
and how much he is patient and doesn't keep score.
So, offer to them the same forgiveness He offers you.
That doesn't mean
You have to open the door and let them back in,
but it means that your heart is no longer being hardened
by what they have put you through.
It means you are no longer
bound by the feelings they made you feel.
Instead, allow God in so He can restore those areas for you,
where anger and bitterness used to reside.
They no longer have a home there.
As He pours and refills you
start to see that the ways others have come at you

is because there is healing in them that they need to do.
Maybe they are not in a space or a place
To start the work,
that's why our love looks different.
Not because it's not offered to them
but because they are too hurt to receive.
So, when I say you will love differently,
That's what I mean.
You will love from a place of understanding.
Healing isn't an overnight thing,
but a journey
One that requires a willing heart and open mind.
All too often you will find
That not everyone is willing to do the work
that is required on the inside.
But when they see you
they will know
that the love you have
is not your love alone.
That you are filled with the love of God.
~End~

Forgive Daily
Forgiving him daily
was like
walking into a war zone.
Where the tension ran high
but God was on my side.
I had a target on my back
with each day bringing new attacks.
But God protected me.
You see
the words that were meant to harm me

and make me cry,
could not penetrate the shield of protection God gave me.
His word says, no weapons formed against you
Shall prosper,
So, He wouldn't let them touch me.
Not even on the days
when I was getting in my feelings.
God swooped in and guarded my gates.
He covered My ears, my mouth, my heart and my eyes.
Not to be touched
by the words that would come out my ex's mouth.
You see
the peace of God
that surpasses all understanding was overflowing in me.
It was in His peace
that I learned to forgive daily.
Not to get caught up by the things I saw,
but to understand
that there was a broken soul that was within
who needed to find Jesus.
And once he did
he would understand God's love.
But until then
I forgive,
Not for him
But for me.
Because God has shown me the love He has
will conquer all.
It's not easy and forgiving may seem hard.
The more that you do it,
you'll start to see the changes made in your heart.
~End~

I Forgive Me Too

I am not perfect
Better yet I'm far from it
But here I am forgiving others
And asking for forgiveness
But having to remember about me too
I forgive me for the things I thought were my fault
I forgive me for the way I have allowed others to treat me
I forgive me for thinking I had to shine away
from the light so others could have a say
I forgive me for the negative self-talk
That I've allowed in my head
I forgive me for not speaking out when I should have
I forgive me for not being the best version of myself
I forgive me for thinking
I was deserving of less
Because the world didn't appreciate
what was on the inside of me
I forgive me too
As I forgive myself
I offer myself grace
Because the weight of all of these things
Are no longer allowed to travel with me
They're too heavy for where I am going
It's time to lay down these burdens at Jesus's feet
Because I can forgive others,
I can forgive me too
~End~

Journal:
Read Luke 7 KJV and pay special attention to the part about the woman Jesus forgave. What did you get out of this story?
What are your thoughts on forgiveness?

Have you asked to be forgiven?

Have you forgiven others and yourself?

What has this journey been like for you?

Prayer

Lord God, forgive me of my sins that may have been done by my words, thoughts, or actions. I ask that you soften my heart to forgive those who have done me wrong. Continue to remind me that I can forgive myself in the process. I thank you for your love that covers a multitude of sins and for your love that doesn't keep score. Make me a heart like yours God, so I can forgive from a deeper place every day. Continue to show me the error of my ways. I no longer want to be held down by the weight of unforgiveness, but to live in the freedom of it's release. In Jesus' name, I humbly pray.

Amen.

Chapter 15

Unpack Your Bags

Come unto me, all ye that labour and are heavy laden, and I
will give you rest. Take my yoke upon you, and learn of me; for I am
meek and lowly in heart: find rest unto your souls. For my yoke is
easy, and my burden is light.
Matthew 11:28-30 KJV

Before you built your relationship with God, you packed your bag based on the things you needed to survive. So, if you had been hungry at one point in your life, your bag would be filled with food, but not enough clothes. You packed based on the things you were used to being in lack of. God is shifting you from surviving to thriving. For that to happen, He has to rewire the way you see your bag of life and then show you how to pack it properly. That may mean, removing some things, throwing some stuff out, and adding some new stuff in. Depending on where you are going, maybe you won't need to bring anything with you, because everything you need will already be there.

This is how it looked in my life. When I was no longer working, I found myself journaling more and more. I was entering into a season of rest which consisted of me learning how to rest in Him. God was pressing me to do the inner work on my soul, He was pulling me to lean into Him more. The baggage of pain I traveled with had become very heavy and it was time to unpack and see all that was inside.

So many memories of my past filled my bag from experiences I had one decade ago and two decades ago. A lot of my current habits were based on things I learned or felt from years ago. Like not feeling I was worthy of receiving good things or feeling obligated to keep certain people in my life because of our history. There was a lot of rewiring that was taking place. The trick of it all was not to get caught up in what I found in my bag. It's okay to sit back and reflect, but not allow it to keep you stuck there back in a place where you feel like you can't move past it. That's not the purpose of the unpacking. It's for you to see what fits and what doesn't so you can make room for the new stuff.

Can you imagine holding on to something you have outgrown only because there was history? The truth is there was no more use for it, but you carried it anyway. God knew there would be things in my bag that no longer suited me and He made provisions for that. He brought exactly what I needed. As I removed things out of my life from my bag it started to get light. What a difference it all made.

Everyone's resting season is going to look different and it may even be different depending on the season you are in. Regardless of where you are in the journey. Trust in Him.

Journal
Soak and listen to worship music for 15 minutes. Ask God to do an inventory check on your life. Ask Him to comb through the people, places and things in your life. Start to get an idea of how much weight you are carrying with you that is not supposed to be there. How much hurt have you been carrying around with you?

Prayer
Lord, expose the people, places and things that need to be removed from my life. Help me to unpack my bag of pain and hurt so that I may make room for you Lord. Show me the steps I need to take so I can continue to follow your path. Thank you for your patience and

love. Thank you for taking the wheel over my life. In Jesus' name, I humbly pray.
Amen.

Chapter 16

Renew Your Mind

*And be not conformed to this world: but be ye transformed by
the renewing of your mind, that ye may prove what is that good, and
acceptable, and perfect, will of God.*
Romans 12:2 KJV

God Give Me Your Mindset
God give me your mindset
so that I can thrive.
Thrive in the purpose you have set inside of me,
once covered by the debris
of lies told by life.
To stop me,
To hinder me,
To keep me,
from opening up my mouth and speaking
the truth about you and all that you do.
Give me your mindset
and cultivate it properly.
Surely
I can handle
the mantle you have designed for me.
I know it's a bit heavy at times,
but as I swiftly move in your grace
I'll be able to handle the pace.
But it takes understanding your mind
to be able to handle the capacity

of what's inside.
Before I can walk in it
I have to be healed and made whole.
Otherwise, your wisdom
would pour out through the holes
of this broken vessel.
People tend to dismiss the power in healing
because they've walked in their hurt for so long.
They think the holes were a part of the original design.
Filled with self-doubt and low self-esteem,
with fear embellished on the rim
unbeknownst to them
it was an unwelcomed addition given by man.
A failed attempt at replacing Your Scripture
with their own plans.
You see
God's mindset
looks past your lack
because there is an abundance
that's supposed to be attached to you.
But somehow it got detached from you
so it's up to God to get you back
into a place
for you to rightfully claim what is yours.
To steward it well
your mind needs to change.
Your mindset of lack will spoil the goods
and there are generations in your bloodline
relying on you.
Get your mind right
so, they too
can steward well
the storehouses being built.

Not just in the physical,
but within themselves.
Building confidence and remaining humble
not leading by pride
are examples
of what leading in love truly looks like.
Get rooted in God's will and operate with His mind
To allow His wisdom in
that He gives away freely from inside
His living word.
The bible has mysteries and strategies
that He will allow you to see
from new angles, you have never seen.
~End~

Use My Story

God will use your story of being broke, broken and abused
to encourage another person to press into their purpose.
Don't think that your stories end right there
because they serve a greater purpose
of more than a distant memory,
you would rather not have to relive.
It is the critical push that another person needs
so they can get back on track to their destiny.
The only way you can do that
is by getting healed and becoming whole
so you can pour into them,
but then also receive
understanding this isn't the end of the road.
but the start of your journey
Giving back to those who are where you were once at
showing them, they are able to conquer their old mindsets.
Watching the chains fall off as they take in the new concepts

That there is a better life that awaits them
once they get through this.
Breakthrough is available
They just have to reach out and grab it
And know that God has made provisions for you to obtain it.
Because the yes you gave to God
Was a yes to every way
that He will use your story
to bring upon another person's healing.
~End~

Journal

What is stopping you from taking a chance on yourself? What is your story? What have you overcome that God is calling you to share for others to get their breakthrough?

Prayer:

Lord, renew my mind within you daily. Continue to show me your ways so that I may walk more like you. Thank you for shifting my mindset and helping me to see how I can be used Show me the areas where work is still needed so that I can have my foundation filled and sealed. Remove any remnants of things that are not of you so I may walk into where you are leading me. Thank you for allowing others to pour into me. I pray that I can do the same. In Jesus' name, I humbly pray.
Amen.

Chapter 17

Stop Trying to Bury Yourself...Again

"There is therefore now no condemnation to them which are in Christ Jesus, who walk not after the flesh, but after the Spirit."
Romans 8:1 KJV

<u>Surrendering Does Not Mean Perfection</u>
When you say yes to God
that does not mean that all your problems stop
or that life will always go well.
It means that you are allowing God to restore you
and use you
for His kingdom.
That means problems will rise,
but you will use the tools that have been refined
to fight a war that you've already won.
It's knowing that mistakes may happen
but there's no condemnation.
Jesus died on the cross and set you free
and because of this, there is provision.
That is not a free pass to be disobedient.
Do not give way into the temptations of the world
because of His grace that is with you.
Simply do your best
to acknowledge Him in all your ways
so He may direct your paths.

As you learn to walk with this time
don't be tempted to put back on the chains
He has already freed you from.
Those chains
Are nothing more than the enemy's way
of tricking you into believing
That your mistakes are grave
and not able to be redeemed.
That's a lie!
From tip the enemy's tongue
sent to confuse you
and move you
10 steps behind.
Because the world has taught you
that the chains are your home.
Instead, live in a state of daily repentance.
Then pray and ask God for a new strategy
to move against the tide of the enemy.
As God places you back into hiding
keeping you safe
He'll pour back into you
what the enemy wanted to take away.
You see the enemy comes to steal, kill and destroy.
He sees you and wants to get to what's inside.
If he can't get to you
He'll do what He can to place doubt inside
of your mind about the gifts God gave you
and about the position, God is calling you to.
So be wary about his design.
Sometimes it comes in sheep's clothing
Trying to hide,
but a wolf can only blend in before being found.
So be discerning about who you are around.

> Pray about everything,
> pray about everyone
> and pray about the words
> that a person may try to speak over you.
> Always confirm with God.
> ~End~

Journal

What is your purpose and are you walking in it?
Have you been able to help others?

Prayer

Lord, I thank you for taking my mess and forming it into a message that serves you and your kingdom. I thank you for allowing me to be able to help other people come from out of their mess so they too can walk in their purpose. I thank you. In Jesus's name, I humbly pray. Amen.

Chapter 18

You are His

For God hath not given us the spirit of fear; but of power, and
of love, and of a sound mind.
2 Timothy 1:7 KJV

You can't allow your wants to come before what God has desired for you. This is going to take self-discipline, but God is there with you every step of the way. This is the unpacking that God does to get to the core areas that concerns you. Fear of the unknown or not fully trusting God can lead to the temptation of wanting to step out of bounds. Know that it is not God who is tempting you and that He has also not given you a spirit of fear.

The more you dive into Him, the easier it becomes to trust and the less likely it is for you to get caught up in the ways of the world. That's not to say mistakes won't happen, but you will recover quicker. The reason is the reassurance God instills in you. It is He, "Who hath saved us and called us with a holy calling, not according to our works, but according to his own purpose and grace, which was given us in Christ Jesus before the world began." (2 Timothy 1: 9 KJV) You were already called by God before time even began. This is God's way of bringing you back to that original stance of why He created you.

Journal
Listen to praise/worship music for 15 minutes. Ask God where He needs you to be more disciplined so that you may be able to complete the assignments, He has given you.

Ask God to build up your confidence as you walk into the calling, He has for you. Be reminded always that as long as He has called you to it, then He is the one who has qualified you for it. That means no one else's validation is needed.

Prayer
Lord I ask that you remove the fear that was once there and refill that void with more of you God. Help me to walk with the power you have instilled in me. May I not be discouraged by the call that you have placed on my life, but be encouraged that you have equipped me for this walk. In Jesus' name, I humbly pray.
Amen.

Chapter 19

The Lord Will Not Tempt You

No temptation has overtaken you except what is common to mankind. And God is faithful; he will not let you be tempted beyond what you can bear. But when you are tempted, he will also provide a way out so that you can endure it.
1 Corinthians 10:13 KJV

Every time I thought I was getting somewhere, an old habit would come up and I would slide back into old ways. It was the most frustrating thing ever. There was a point when God was ministering to my spirit as to why certain habits were harder for me to kick out of my life. In those talks, He showed me that He didn't love me any less. It was Him giving me an opportunity to exercise my trust and learn to call on Him in my moments of weakness. I would sit back and run through the course of events and see how God was intervening for me, but it was on me to take the help.

Sometimes there are temptations that sneak up on us and then there are those that we walk right into. These could be anything from drinking alcohol, running back to an ex-partner, having sex, or whatever it is that you are working on resisting. It's important to be mindful of where you are in your journey and not purposely put yourself in situations that you have no business being in. It's true that life happens and mistakes are made, but don't go looking to walk the line of fire if you don't have to.

Journal

Write down any areas of temptations you have now or one that you have been able to get over? How were you able to overcome that temptation?

Prayer

Lord, you continue to be my rock regardless of what I may be going through. You continue to show up even in the midst of temptations. Although I may not always get it right, I thank you for your saving grace. Help me in the areas to be strong where I am weak. Reveal unto me the areas where work is still needed. Help me to continue to grow my trust and faith in you. Please forgive me father and cleanse my heart. I just want to serve you and do what you have asked me to do. Expand my capacity to be okay with getting uncomfortable because there is a great work taking place in me. In Jesus' name I humbly pray. Amen.

<u>Sick</u>

You want to talk about turning to the things that made me sick.
How many times
Did I find myself repeating the same steps over and over?
How many times did I experience that same cycle?
How many times did I have to endure the same thing?
Little did I know there was protection in the cycle.
He was keeping me and providing me an opportunity
to advance, to learn and to be in His presence.
He cared enough to keep me still and to move strategically.
So many questions came to mind,
But not enough to make me want to be seen.
~End~

Part III

Revived

Chapter 20

It all Works for Your Good

"And we know that all things work together for good to them
that love God, to them who are the called according to his
purpose."
Romans 8:28 KJV

Have you ever stayed at a job longer than you should have? I did and because of that, I found myself being let go because the job no longer suited me. My manager whom I knew for five years was upset that I had gained a lot of respect and influence from my peers that he did not have. He was not a fan of it and felt it best for me to be let go. I had gotten so comfortable with this job that I didn't realize I had outgrown it.

So instead of looking at the blessing in being let go, I was walking in hurt, anger and betrayal. It took me two years to realize that if I had stayed there, my growth would have been stunted. I would have remained stagnant in an environment that no longer offered an area of growth for me.

During this healing journey, God told me that not every betrayal was surface deep. It was the betrayals I experienced that ushered me onto my path of purpose. This could only be accomplished if I was willing to let go of some people, places and things. It was an uncomfortable process, but it was a checkpoint I needed to pass through for me to grow.

God used that hurt and pain as fuel to thrust me forward. As I propelled into new opportunities, God was working in the background. He knew that I wouldn't immediately understand so He made provisions on my behalf. It wasn't until the appointed time that I was able to grasp why things happened the way they did. This revelation moved me from being angry and hurt to being overjoyed. What God has for me is far bigger than what that job could ever provide me. There was a light within me that couldn't shine as bright where I was. I had to be removed for the shade to be removed from it.

Betrayal Ushered Me In

Allow that betrayal to thrust you into your next.
Your next opportunity
or your next big break.
Allow God to mend your broken heart
and heal you from the pain.
There is a purpose of the things you have to let go of.
There are better things ahead.
Places and positions that God wants to promote you to,
but how do you get there
if you are not willing to change.
It may look scary
and you might not have it all planned
but if God is leading you to it
Then it has to work.
He is above all
and He is able to make the impossible possible.
When God says He will use all things,
Trust that He will.
It will be done in a way that
you couldn't even put into words.
The question to you is,
do you trust Him?

Do you trust Him to take you from where you are
to where He is calling you to be?
Do you trust Him to provide a way for you and your family?
Do you trust that He has created a way when all hope seems
lost?
I need you to trust that you have truly been called
and hand-selected from among the rest.
But will you follow?
Will you allow Him to lead you to the next place?
May God open your mind and soften heart
so that you may be able to receive the new things
that He is getting ready to do for you.
He will take all that you have been through
and use it to usher you through
on the other side of trusting Him
Is your breakthrough
With all the promises God has laid out for you.
~End~

Journal

Listen to worship/praise music for 15 minutes. Ask God to bring you the clarity you need on some of the betrayals or rejections you have faced. Write down what comes to mind, including what you see and hear. Reflect on the moments that are coming to your mind. Allow God to love on you during this time.

Prayer

Heavenly Father, I thank you for always being my side even in the midst of storms. I thank you for protecting me and the light you have placed inside of me even when I couldn't see what was going on. I thank you for being in control and making all things work out for my good. I thank you for healing my heart and providing the clarity that I needed to forgive myself and others so that I could move on. I thank

you for always showing up for me regardless of how things may look. You are always there. Right by my side, every step of the way. It's in Jesus' name, I humbly pray.
Amen.

Chapter 21

Rooted in God

"That we henceforth be no more children, tossed to and fro,
and carried about with every wind of doctrine, by the sleight of men,
and cunning craftiness, whereby they lie in wait to deceive"
Ephesians 4:14 KJV

<u>Rooted</u>

Your roots
Have they been buried this time?
Or are they still shallow deep?
I mean, what's inside of me
that wants to keep uprooting this tree?
It's like saying it's too cold so,
I'm going to move it to a different spot.
It's too hot here
Something isn't quite right.
Where do I put it?
It needs to be in soil
But where's the right place?
In my mind the elements outside
are too much for my precious tree.
But I know that if I don't plant it somewhere
it's going to die.
Not from the elements
but because of me being me confused.
Confused about the placement,
but there are other trees
that are here.

And they've done just fine
So why am I worried?
They endured cold winters and hot summers.
They have seen storms and snow.
Still, they thrive and
fruits are produced each season.
So why am I so worried
about my tree?
Is it because it's young?
But were these trees not once seeds?
Learning early to dig their roots in deep.
There's a reason roots go down into the earth
and not rest above the ground.
If they rested above,
they would leave themselves vulnerable to sway and swing
around.
So, do you trust Him to nourish you as He has done for the
older trees?
Providing you protection even in unfavorable elements
trusting the process to provide sweet fruit from it.
The question that lies in your heart
is will he do the same for me
As He has done for them?
The answer is simple.
Yes, He will.
As long as you allow your roots to run deep
you will see that you are rooted in solid ground.
When the wind picks up,
do not be alarmed
or go back into old habits of pulling yourself out.
Instead, dive in a bit deeper.
Deeper into your anchor,
like a scared child who holds on tighter.

~End~

Journal
Soak and worship for 15 minutes. Ask God to show you how you are rooted in Him and how to dig your roots in deeper. Write down everything that comes to mind including what you hear and see.

Prayer
Lord I ask that you help me to remain rooted in you regardless of what happens in my life. I ask that even when curve balls get thrown me way to take me off track that you swiftly realign me back in to position. Thank you for being patient with my growth. In Jesus' name, I humbly pray.
Amen.

Chapter 22

The New Place

Enter into his gates with thanksgiving, and into his courts with
praise: be thankful unto him, and bless his name.
Psalm 100:4 KJV

<u>Welcome to the New</u>
I encourage you to steward your new season well
by staying at the feet of Jesus
To be filled up like a well.
Shine your light on others.
Be the vessel God called you to be.
Shine bright
Because you are being ushered into your
new place, new position, new mindset
and new version of you.
One that others have not seen before.
Some may not even recognize you
and that's the point
Who you are now,
should not reflect who you once were.
It's your past that we use
to go and save souls
to show them that there is hope
to move past their pain.
A an example to others
that they don't have to live the same.
They can live a new way

if they choose to surrender today.
Give it all back to God and allow Him back in
to make a huge change from within.
There's still a choice you have to make,
to let go of the wheel.
Because even in the new place
the enemy is real.
Don't get distracted by all that's new.
Seek God daily,
so He can continue to move through you.
~End~

God uprooted what He needed to and dug up the past to release me from many things. I now had room to grow in a healthy environment. I was beyond thankful for that. I could feel myself taking root in God in more areas as I learned new things about myself. As my roots received nourishment from Him, I was able to start breaking through my shell. The seeds in me were starting to finally grow. I would be able to bear fruits for me and many generations to come.

Embracing the journey meant celebrating both the small and big wins. An attitude of gratitude shifts your perspective on the outward lens of life and it lessens the pressure placed on yourself. I could finally look up and realize that I was no longer in the same spot that I once was in. I had been moved to a new place. One that has others who are flourishing right in front of me. I was not alone. Although, I could not see them when I was buried under the pain, I was able to see them now. On the other side of it all. So many others had been where I was and they too had been replotted to be revived.

Journal

What are some promises God has given you? Continue to review these daily to remind yourself what God is doing for you in your life.

Prayer
God I bless you for the journey. Especially for your patience when I couldn't understand what was going on. I thank you for being with me every step of the way. I ask that you continue to reveal to me my purpose so that I may be able to help others along their journey. I thank you for removing the weeds, digging up my past and reviving me. In Jesus' humble name, I pray.
Amen.

Chapter 23

See The Change Within

Romans 15:13 KJV
Now unto him that is able to do exceeding abundantly above all
that we ask or think, according to the power that worketh in us,

In the Blink of an Eye a Year Passed By
The last 365 days have been the ride
of a lifetime.
I had to come from underneath
all the pain life threw my way.
That's almost 3 decades worth of
pain, rejection and blame.
I mean it was all the yucky stuff
And all the stuff that I even thought was okay
that I needed deliverance from.
Areas that I needed to sit down my pride and humble myself
To receive the healing
And become whole
In every nook and cranny within my soul.
I needed Jesus
to save me and keep me
from going back into the chains of slavery
in my mind and of my past.
I had to stay rooted in God
so the enemy couldn't have the last laugh.
Or even a final thought in anything
concerning the way,

that God was working in me.
It was a year of tears and fighting.
It was a year of self-love and rebuilding.
It was a year of trusting and relying on God.
A year of no longer being able to lean on myself.
Learning to understand the power of forgiveness
and walking in love through it all.
Relinquishing my control
and my need to know
what was happening next in front of me.
Truly having faith in God and letting go
of the things the world taught me.
I unlearned old habits while God rewired my brain
To believing in me more
so when others saw me
they'll know I'm not the same.
Because my identity was no longer
tied to the world,
but to Jesus Christ our Lord.
When you know who are in Him
your self-worth goes up and
your value changes.
Nothing about you is able to be the same.
There is a Godfidence that roars from deep inside
and anything that is not of God
will have to come outside.
Because they will know that you have learned your name.
You will be a force to be reckoned with
because you stand on His name.
To those who don't believe,
I promise you this is not a game
there is a transformation
being requested of you in this hour.

Will you go forth and take His hand,
So you can then take your rightful place?
~End~

Take a Walk with Me

When I started this journey,
I was broken down, lost and confused.
I was angry at a situation I didn't choose
No one turns 29 expecting to lose
a relationship they invested a decade into.
Buried by the weight of my life
I couldn't see past the strife
that I walked in on a daily basis.
Unaware that the source of this
was from unforgiveness.
From a job that let me go two years ago
but it goes to show
that our experiences shape the way we think, walk and talk.
Sometimes we see it
but if you've walked in it long enough
you can barely tell the difference.
I didn't know the path I was going on
would bring me through the fire of hard truths
while I waited on You to fulfill
the healing You promised me.
Uncomfortable rounds of uncovering my misery
led to checking in with you for the next steps,
while there were days you only told me to rest.
I would be frustrated at not knowing what you meant
and upset with myself because I kept failing the same test.
I was unaware that it was a journey
to build up my strength.
I wanted it to be perfect and I was far from it.

I was hard on myself
and set unrealistic expectations
He didn't even ask for.
All you said was to
show up, trust and do the work.
It sounds simple enough,
But it was tough.
There were curves balls life threw my way
Having to stand tall in the midst of it all.
Your growth in God
is seen how you react to old situations
and things that once made you bent out of shape.
You'll start to see how you slow down
to analyze your day
and the ways where things could have gone a different way.
~End~

This last year was one of the hardest years I experienced mentally, emotionally and spiritually. Yet, I was able to overcome it all by the grace of God. God had placed amazing people in my life. Some were there from the very start of the chaos and others were there for different seasons to pour encouraging words into me. So, I thank God for pushing me when I wanted to just curl up on some days because it felt like a never-ending cycle.

Today I can say that I am on the other side of my pain. Healed and becoming whole as I embrace all of whom God created me to be. I am going to continue living my life boldly for God in every way I can. At turns when there seemed to be no way out, God showed up and made a way for me. There were days that life piled everything on top of me from dealing with my children, to my household, to being able to provide for them. It was a lot and on some days it almost became overwhelming, but God. He showed up and kept me.

Even now life continues providing it's fair share of challenges my way, but because I have renewed my mind in Christ, I don't look at them the same. I know what my tools are and where my strength comes from. I know that if God is allowing me through it, provisions have been made for it. So I continue to worship and give Him praise; because on the not-so-great days, there is a blessing He has provides me with. I just have to be willing to look and find it.

Journal
Listen to praise and worship music for 15 minutes. Ask God where He needs you this season and how you can live your life boldly for Him. Write down what comes to mind including what you see and hear.

Prayer
Lord, I thank you. I thank you for the healing you have done and will continue to do in me. I thank you for strengthening my roots so that they continue to dive deeper into you. I thank you for the boldness you have placed in me and I ask that I carry that boldness everywhere I go. Continue to protect me and walk before me. Show me the areas where I need to be humbled and soften my heart so it can be more like yours. Thank you for keeping me through everything I have endured. In Jesus' name, I humbly pray.
Amen.

About the Author

I am your transformation coach Jessica Harris and I am the visionary founder of Ignite UR Glow, LLC. I'm also a transformation speaker, blogger, podcaster and more. Most importantly I am the mom to three mini versions of myself who I always say don't look like me, but act like me sometimes.

I invite you to check out my other work: *Live a Life of Gratitude Journal, See the Beauty from Within Affirmations Journal, Dear God: A journal for hope, love and strength* and *Believe Again Prayer Journal.* I am currently working on a series of eBooks for entrepreneurs that will be launching soon. So follow me on Instagram @igniteurglow for more releases. Follow me at @ignite_ur_glow for more on my journey of transformation and transforming others. If you are a focus-driven women, then I want to extend you the offer of joining the Ignite UR Glow movement. We are breaking down the barriers of self-limiting belief systems, old mindsets and more so we can walk confidently in the purpose God has placed inside of us.

Let's Connect Further:
- Website: www.igniteurglow.com
- Instagram: @ignite_ur_glow and @igniteurglow
- Email: igniteurglow@gmail.com